FIRST GRACES

Illustrated by
TASHA TUDOR

The Lutterworth Press

First published in Great Britain, 1964

This impression 1991

L

The Lutterworth Press
P.O. Box 60
Cambridge CB1 2NT
England

ISBN 0 7188 0307 8

Printed in Hong Kong by Colorcraft Ltd

TO
POLLY THAYER STARR
WITH LOVE AND
GRATITUDE

Dear Lord, I offer Thee this day
All I shall think, or do, or say.

T. Tudor

For food, and all Thy gifts of love,
    We give Thee thanks and praise.
Look down, O Father, from above
    And bless us all our days.

T. Tudor
1955

For what we are about to receive,
the Lord make us truly thankful.

T. Tudor
1955

Some hae meat, and canna eat,
   And some wad eat that want it;
But we hae meat and we can eat,
   And sae the Lord be thankit.

Robert Burns

T. Tudor

For every cup and plateful,
God make us truly grateful.
A. S. T. Fisher

Bless, O Lord, this food to our use,

And us to Thy loving service.

God, we thank You for this food,
For rest and home and all things good;
For wind and rain and sun above,
But most of all for those we love.

Maryleona Frost

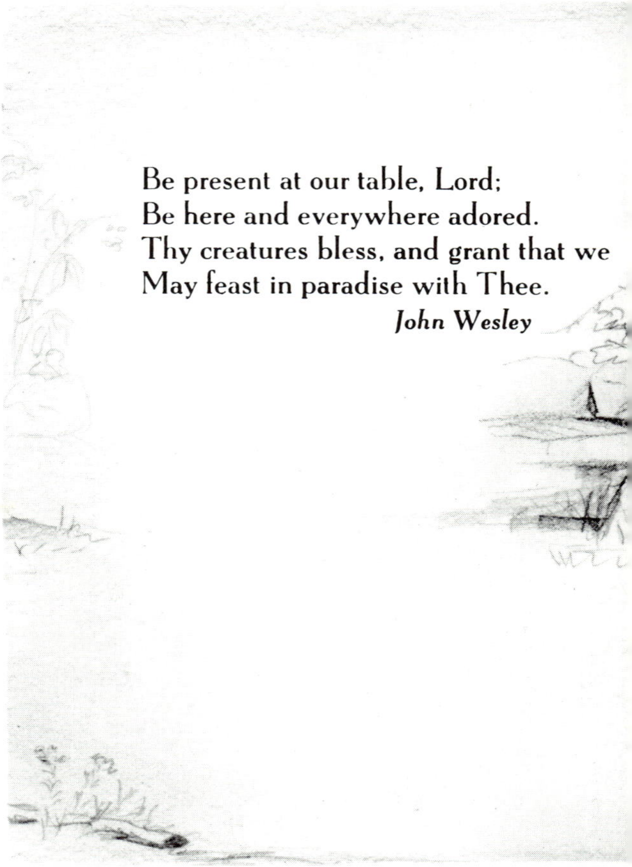

Be present at our table, Lord;
Be here and everywhere adored.
Thy creatures bless, and grant that we
May feast in paradise with Thee.

John Wesley

T. Tudor
1955

We thank Thee, Lord, for happy hearts,
For rain and sunny weather.
We thank Thee, Lord, for this our food,
And that we are together.

Emilie Fendall Johnson

T. Tudor

Jesus, friend of little children,
Be a friend to me;
Take my hand and ever keep me
Close to Thee.

Walter J. Mathans

The Lord my pasture shall prepare,
And feed me with a shepherd's care;
His presence shall my wants supply,
And guard me with a watchful eye.

Joseph Addison

T. Tudor

At the New Year

Thanks be to Thee, Lord Jesus,
For another year to serve Thee,
To love Thee,
And to praise Thee.

T. Tudor
1955

A Birthday Grace

God made the sun
  And God made the tree,
God made the mountains
  And God made me.

I thank You, O God,
For the sun and the tree,
For making the mountains
And for making me.

Leah Gale

At Easter

Joyfully, this Easter day,
I kneel, a little child, to pray;
Jesus, who hath conquered death,
Teach me, with my every breath,
To praise and worship Thee.

Sharon Banigan

Springtime

All things bright and beautiful,
All creatures great and small,
All things wise and wonderful,
The Lord God made them all.

Each little flower that opens,
Each little bird that sings,
He made their glowing colours,
He made their tiny wings.

Mrs. C. F. Alexander

For School

At home or at school
Wherever I may go
One thought I remember
That is good to know.
It stays in my heart
A happy little song
That God takes care of me
The whole day long.

J. Lilian Vandevere

T. Tudor

For the beauty of the earth,
For the beauty of the skies,
For the love which from our birth
Over and around us lies,

For the beauty of each hour,
Of the day and of the night,
Hill and vale, and tree and flower,
Sun and moon, and stars of light,

Gracious God, to Thee we raise
This our sacrifice of praise.

F. S. Pierpoint

T. Tudor

Thank You for the world so sweet,
Thank You for the food we eat,
Thank You for the birds that sing,
Thank You, God, for everything.

E. Rutter Leatham

Thanksgiving

May God give us grateful hearts
And keep us mindful
Of the need of others.

T. Tudor

Christmas Eve

What can I give Him,
  Poor as I am?
  If I were a shepherd,
I would bring a lamb;
  If I were a wise man,
  I would do my part;
But what I can I give Him!
  Give my heart.

Christina Rossetti

Christmas Day

Glory to God in the highest,
and on earth peace,
good will toward men.

Luke 2:14

T. Tudor

WE OFFER sincere thanks to the various publishers and copyright holders for permission to reprint; "Dear Lord, I offer thee this day" from *Prayers for All Occasions*, Forward Movement Publications of the Episcopal Church; "For food, and all thy gifts of love" from *A Little Book of Prayers and Graces*, by Quail Hawkins, illustrated by Marguerite de Angeli; copyright 1941, 1952 by Doubleday & Co., Inc.; "For every cup and plateful" from *An Anthology of Prayers*, by A. S. T. Fisher, copyright 1934 by Longmans, Green & Co.; "God, we thank you for this food," by Maryleona Frost, *Wee Wisdom*; "We thank thee, Lord, for happy hearts" from *A Little Book of Prayers*, by Emilie Fendall

Johnson, copyright 1941 by the author and Maud and Miska Petersham, The Viking Press, Inc., New York; "Thanks be to thee, Lord Jesus" from *Prayers for Members of the Holy Family*, Diocese of Pittsburgh; "God made the sun" from *Prayers for Children*, copyright 1942 by Simon & Schuster, Inc., and the Artists and Writers Guild, Inc.; "Joyfully, this Easter Day" from *Hear Our Prayer*, by Sharon Banigan, copyright 1946 by S. E. Lowe, Inc., Kenosha; "At home or at school" from *Our First Music*, C. C. Birchard & Co.; "Thank you for the world so sweet "by E. Rutter Leatham, copyright holder Mrs. Lorna Hill.